The Prodigal Father

Father

UNDERSTANDING GOD'S RECKLESS LOVE

CRAIG OMOROTIONMWAN

THE PRODIGAL FATHER

Rev Craig Ministries
+234 818 885 7772

ISBN: 978-978-967-526-5

Published by:

PRINTING
AND PUBLICATIONS
COMPANY LTD

Benson Idahosa University Campus,
Ugbor Road, G.R.A., Benin City.
0813 9499 779, 0816 2410 122, 0902 6853 932
Email: aboveonlypress@gmail.com

Endorsements

Dear Chris, God loves you recklessly

The story of the prodigal Father is the story of a Father's love which forms the core of the gospel of Christ.

Forgiveness is at the heart of it. Throughout the bible the teaching of love and forgiveness in Christ is central:

God gives His all to us and has cleared us of all wrongdoing through the sacrifice of Christ. In Him we obtain repeated opportunities to live our lives as favoured children of an indulgent Father.

In this timely book, Rev. Craig Omorotionmwan clearly showcases the love that God our Father has for us in the cross of Jesus, and His love chases out all fear. When you were a sinner, God loved you; much more so now that you are His own. God can never be angry with the one who has put his faith in Jesus because he has gone as far as killing for you. All His anger over your sin and error came on Jesus on the cross. Your sin is dealt with and is no longer a hindrance to you drawing near to God. He loves you; you are forgiven and free from all fear.

I believe everyone should read this book and become grounded in God's love to enjoy a life of grace without fear.

I've known Rev. Craig for years now, he has been a great blessing to me and Savannah ministries, ministering in our Camp meeting in the UK. He is a great and anointed teacher of God's word, and this book will be a great blessing to all.

Rev. Arome Adah
G.O
Savannah Ministries
www.savannahministries.org

Rev Craig has penned an awesome material that I would first recommend to be adopted in every discipleship content on the assurance of salvation.

Secondly, I recommend this book to all who bear the oracle of God on the crucial need to be gracious with the message of the cross.

Thirdly, this is a must read for anyone who desires to consistently live a victorious life as a child of God.

Rev. Opara Emmanuel.
President, The CORE ministry,
Director at, Rare virtue consulting

Timely and riveting! A must read for every believer. Rev. Craig turns the table around on the most beloved parable of the scripture and shows us the Father as the guilty party of love. This simple approach provides a foundation and the building blocks of every believer's faith.

Reigner Davies
College Director, MouldBreak learning community.

Rev. Craig is an able minister of the New Testament with a humble heart of love and the tangible power of the Spirit. He pours out his heart as he expounds on the Lord's love as revealed in the parable of the Prodigal Father. The message remains as refreshing and compelling as when I first heard him teach it some years ago. This book is a treasure trove; a joy to many generations. The book is bound to heal you, realign your perspective and above all; help you experience the boundless love that Jesus Christ has for you.

Moyo Akin-ojo
Manifold Grace Ministries

Contents

Contents

Foreword

For so many years, Craig has been a very dear son to me and I am indeed very proud of him. In this wonderful book – 'The Prodigal Father', Craig shares a very powerful Christ centered exposition of the entire chapter of Luke 15. With vast historical details and deep revelational insight, he paints a very interesting and clear picture of the extravagant love of God the Father; the very love that Jesus fully personified and longs for us to grasp and reflect in its entirety. So many sinners and believers alike, have a very wrong notion about God; owing to many wrong things they have heard about God, but I really thank God for how he is using many vessels like Craig to sound and proclaim the gospel of His grace like never before.

In this wonderful book, Craig also talks about the right attitude we are to have towards sinners if we are going to be able to reach them like Jesus did when He was on the earth. He lays a lot of emphasis on placing great value on one soul like God does and passionately reaching out and not giving up till we find and get the lost into the great love of the Father. In reading the third parable in Luke 15, many are tempted to focus and think that the emphasis is on the son who took his share of his father's wealth and went to squander it; but the focus and emphasis is actually on how unbelievably loving the father is, just like God the Father is to us all.

We are in a new day! The day that Psalm 118 verse 24 says the Lord has made that we are to rejoice in, is not a 24-hour period, but a new dispensation that has been brought about by the death, burial and resurrection of Christ. One major attribute of this day that we are in, is we have entered God's Rest. We no longer have to struggle in our own efforts to impress God. God is already impressed with us and He has made us righteous by the works of Jesus. Believing in your works to make you righteous or accepted by God actually makes God angry because you are telling Him that you do not value all that He did for you in Christ. It is only when you are at rest that God can work in your life. Resting in God by having faith in the works of Jesus for you, makes you experience the miraculous power and abundance of God in your life.

By the sacrifice of Jesus for us on the Cross, all our sins are forgiven. I don't mean just the sins of the believer alone, but the sins of the whole world. Jesus is the Lamb of God that takes away the sins of the world and He has taken all our sins away (past, present and future) by His death on the Cross.

As a just God, God hates sin and sin must be

punished, so God put all our sins on Jesus and credited us with His righteousness. God is no longer angry with you because He has put all of His anger upon Jesus. He wants you to receive His forgiveness and embrace His love. Now does this in any way mean that we can now continue to live in sin? No, not at all. This is what makes us love God and want to please Him more. Psa.130:3-4 says "If You, Lord, should mark iniquities, O Lord, who could stand? But there is forgiveness with You, That You may be feared." It is not the terror of God that makes us reverence Him, but the love and forgiveness of God. It is only when you truly understand God's love towards you that you will be able to rest in Him and also reflect that same love unto others. God is not a wicked and angry God waiting to punish us but a dear and loving Father eagerly extending His extravagant love towards us.

It is my earnest prayer that as you read this book, you will come out of every fearful slave mentality you may have had towards God the Father and come into the faith, love and joy filled sonship consciousness that God wants you to have towards Him. I pray that you will embrace the grace and love of God like never before and you will be free to live the abundant and victorious life that God has provided for you in Christ. You will also love and reach out to others with the amazing love of God the Father.

Rev. Wale Ajayi,
Senior Pastor,
CGMI Miracle Centre, Benin City.

Introduction

I hurried home that day after school, entered my room and shut the door firmly behind me. Promptly getting on my knees, I made this earnest, heartfelt prayer to God; "Father, I am truly sorry that I was too hasty to receive Jesus, I only just realized that I had not counted the cost. I take back my words of commitment to being born again and hereby renounce that I'm a Christian. Do give me some time to work on myself before coming back to you. But just in case Jesus comes pretty soon as we all expect him to, I think it will be safer to go to hell as an unbeliever so my part of hell won't be too hot"

As a young Christian in secondary school, I was told that if I ever sinned again after receiving Jesus into my heart, God would blot out my name from the book of life. In addition to that, God would ensure that I was put in the hottest part of hell, because I once received the light of salvation and then turned around and sinned. I was also made to believe that a sinner who had never received Christ would be better off than me; and their place in hell will not be so hot since they never knew Jesus.

Funny as this may sound, it is a true story. It is the true story of how my dread for God began, and took its toll on me for many years to come. The same is true for many people today; somehow, they have bought into the notion that God is a strict, no nonsense ruler who has set stringent rules for his subjects to follow, or face dire consequences. There is the belief that after you become born again, God raises the bar and tones down his affection to an all-time low. Many feel it is difficult to measure up to God's standards and expectations of us, "Christianity is hard" they say. Yet Jesus said that for those who labour and are heavy laden, he would grant rest. (Matthew 11:28). He surely was not talking about being laid to rest in a sorry tomb of depression and condemnation. He was talking about easing the burden of religion. We have not received the spirit that brings us into bondage again to fear, (Romans 8:15); that makes us afraid to relate to God as a Father. We have not received a spirit that makes us afraid of God.

At the heart of this book is a strong message that addresses that fear, and clearly demonstrates that if God so loved us while we were sinners, and far away from Him, then he loves us even much more, now that we have come home to Him. **"But God has made clear his love to us, in that, when we were still sinners, Christ gave his life for us. Much more, if we now have righteousness by his blood, will salvation from the wrath of God come to us through him. For if, when** we were haters of God, the death of his son made us at peace with him, much more, now that we are his friends, will we have salvation through his life" (Romans 5:8-10. Bible in Basic English Translation.)

The mindset of God as taskmaster is an offspring of the message that is devoid of God's love. It breeds fear and sends faith out the door. It turns the faith that moves mountains into an insurmountable mountain itself that prevents us from reaching our Father. Whereas a clear understanding of the Father's undying love for us will cast out all fear from our hearts. **"Such love has no fear, because perfect love expels all fear. If we are afraid, it is for fear of punishment, and this shows that we have not fully experienced his perfect love".** (New Living Translation). This love supplies to us the needed confidence to approach God and call him; Daddy!

Chapter 1

Wine and Dine Outreach

What stirred the waters was a simple gesture extended to a group of dedicated sinners.

They came to Jesus to hear him talk. Two things were involved; firstly, what he had to say must have been interesting. Luke 15:1 says that Publicans and Sinners came to hear him. The Greek word translated sinners, is "hamartolos" and it means "devoted to sin". Trust me, it takes much more than some fiery and judgmental religious speech to get this notorious pack crawling unto repentance. They do not quit the sinning business that easy; most of them have already considered the possible consequences of sin and damned it. Once when John the Baptist preached a fiery message, the majority of those driven to repentance, for fear of the wrath to come, were the Pharisees and the Sadducees (Mark 3:7). But what Jesus preached was the year or season of God's acceptance; He said he was sent to preach the acceptable year of the Lord" (Luke 4:19) When Jesus was before sinners, he was nothing like John the Baptist. His most scathing rebukes were reserved for the self-righteous folks of his day.

You would be greatly mistaken to think that Jesus was archaic and old fashioned. Let me either remind you or bring to your notice, that Jesus was a youth. He had just crossed his twenties and was somewhere in his very early thirties when this event occurred. It will be therefore safe to assume that his youthfulness played some role in his delivery; and definitely not with a diluting effect. If we do not take this into cognizance, then we will be doing much injustice, by our faulty perception, to the person and character of the man Jesus, as regards his life on earth. Secondly, he taught them "… as one that had authority, and not as the scribes (teachers of the law) Matthew 7:29."

The stereotyped and inflexible mindset of the biblical Pharisaical bunch, as well as that of the scribes, were manifest in their vehement disapproval of Jesus' method of outreach. *"…This man welcomes sinners and eats with them"* (Luke 15:2, New International Version). The religious leaders of the day had zero tolerance for sinners; you were either for them or against them, with them or separate from them.

But Jesus mingled. He would rather offend the religious rulers than offend sinners. He even ate with them. Rich sinners, as these possibly were, sure knew how to enjoy a good meal. They didn't go to Jesus on empty; they came with sumptuous meals; so Jesus was having a good meal on a good day with the bad guys, and then, the religious leaders show up! Bad timing! The atmosphere was fouled from their horrid looks. His crime? He had allowed sinners into his space.

The admonition to "…come out from among them and be ye separate" (2 Corinthians 6:17) is not a call to avoid relating with sinners, but an appeal not to partake with them in their evil. Why should we avoid the very people we have been sent to reach out for? Our sanctimonious habitude towards unbelievers invariably keeps us worlds apart from them. It is my firm belief that as believers, we must strategize on how to break into their circles with the love of Christ. Jesus sent us to go into all the world to preach the good news. It is imperative that we wear the gracious aura of the gospel message, that unique flavour that is peculiar to the good news of Jesus. No more should it be thought a thing of pride and virtue that sinners are convicted of their sins at our appearing. That will be going much farther than the Holy Spirit Himself; for He does not convict the world of their sins (plural) but of their sin (singular). (John 16:8-9). The only sin that the Holy Spirit convicts the world of is the sin of not believing in Jesus. When they encounter us, let them see the face of a loving God whose kindness calls them to repentance. To present Him as an angry God is to betray His person and character. We are required to be faithful stewards who portray the heart of the Father. For too long many have painted a grotesque caricature of God and made him "most unwanted".

Jesus was neither perturbed nor fazed by the unsolicited intrusion and murmurings of the Pharisees and Scribes. Stretching his hand towards his sinner friends, he doused their rising tempers; gently swallowed the food in his mouth, and sipped a little drink. Then with a flush of peace in his soul, and the resulting calmness in his demeanor, he lifted his face from the dining table, and responded to his critics in parables.

Chapter 2

Go in Search Until...

Israel was an agrarian community, and sheep were greatly priced. The Jewish leaders certainly knew the value of sheep. So Jesus first parable begins as a rhetorical question, but with pretty interesting details. Luke 15:4 *"What man of you, having a hundred sheep, if he has lost one of them, does not leave the ninety-nine in the wilderness, and go after the one which is lost, until he finds it?"* (Revised Standard Version). It is evident from his presentation that this was generally expected from shepherds in his day, and to deviate from this pattern of response in the event that a sheep got missing, would be most insensitive and heartless, to say the least. "Which man of you will be heartless enough to abandon even one lost sheep? Which one of you will dare be satisfied enough with the many sheep left in the pen, as to neglect the one that is lost?" By this question, Jesus accentuates his resolve to seek and to save the lost. He draws the middle very clearly before the religious leaders, taking his stand across, while set over against them. The same question goes to you precious readers; which one of you Pastors is satisfied with your sizeable congregation as to no longer care about reaching out to the lost? Which one of you is comfortable being a Christian and groans no more within when even one member of your family, colleague at work or friends, has not received the light of this glorious gospel? Do we pride ourselves over them saying "well, they don't know what we enjoy in Christ". Jesus is asking the same question today, "which man among you..."

Here, Jesus highlights the value of one soul. The shepherd leaves the ninety-nine and goes in search of that sheep UNTIL he finds it. First, he leaves the convenience of the company of the ninety-nine lot and begins a search for the missing sheep. This is a deliberate effort, not some nonchalant search around for a white furred mass lying somewhere in the corner. This kind was a rigorous search; first the shepherd would begin counting while leading them one after the other into the pen. Sometimes he would miss his count when a few sheep rush in to enter at the same time. Then he'll assume a number in his mind and continue counting. If the number did not sum up to a hundred after counting, he would assume that the earlier rush of the sheep made him miss his count. He would then lead them out of the pen while counting afresh. This process would be repeated until a consistent number is realized. If it was then confirmed that one of the sheep was missing, then the shepherd would go back along every path he had earlier led the whole flock to graze. He would have to check by every stream he had led them to drink and refresh themselves. He would have to climb back up on every mountain he had led them. He would have to go around every mountain to see if the sheep was trapped in one of the cracks.

How quickly do we give up on that unsaved neighbour? How long do we stay on that incorrigible drug addict? How long do we persevere in love with that disgraceful sibling? Or are we embarrassed at the stain that their lifestyles bring upon our impeccable integrity? Do we disdain and reject them in our hearts wishing they were not our relative? Do we cringe from being identified with them in public to avoid denting our super reputation amongst people? Where does this stem from? Is it not from self-righteous pride; the kind that makes us rejoice over the one we feel we are better than? Surely it is.

Self-righteousness numbs our hearts to ailing sinners. In Luke 18:10-14, Jesus tells the story of two men who went into the temple to pray; one a Pharisee and the other a publican otherwise known as a sinner. The Pharisee promptly began his prayers by comparing himself with others and with the publican: *"God I thank you that I am not as other men are, extortionists, unjust, adulterers, or even as this publican".*

It is a spiritual vice to attempt to get ones' self-worth by marking another person's shortcoming. When we do this we can never attain to our full potential because we are always only as good as another person is bad. Our competence and effectiveness is measured not by the performance of another, but by the inner God given capacity and potential we possess, and by how well we engage and translate them into visible reality. Quit trying to get your sense of value from another person's failure. Run your own race and make your own impact. Self-righteousness **makes** you focus on the little you have done or are doing, all the while blinded to what you ought to be doing.

The Pharisee went on to say in his prayer: *"I fast twice a week, I give tithes of all that I possess"* Self-righteousness cripples your love walk; it thrives on seeing others as beneath you. Then you would do nothing to see people around you improve for fear that you might lose you relevance and occasion for boasting.

Self-righteousness causes us to get offended at the sinner for his reluctance or refusal to come to Christ. Some even begin to boast about how early, or how quickly in life they made a decision for Jesus when they heard the gospel. They boast about how quickly they gave up their bad habits. But if we must reach the lost at all cost, then we must have the patient heart of Jesus. Receive this counsel from Philippians 2:4-11 (Message Bible)

"Don't push your way to the front; don't sweet-talk your way to the top. Put yourself aside, and help others get ahead. Don't be obsessed with getting your own advantage. Forget yourselves long enough to lend a helping hand. Think of yourselves the way Christ Jesus thought of himself. He had equal status with God but didn't think so much of himself that he had to cling to the advantages of that status no matter what. Not at all. When the time came, he set aside the privileges of deity and took on the status of a slave, became human! Having become human, he stayed human. It was an incredibly humbling process. He didn't claim special privileges. Instead, he lived a selfless, obedient life and then died a selfless obedient death – and the worst kind of death at that – a crucifixion. Because of that obedience, God lifted him high and honored him far beyond anyone or anything, ever, so that all created beings in heaven and on earth – even those long dead and buried – will bow in worship before this Jesus Christ, and call out in praise

that he is the Master of all, to the glorious honor of God the Father"

The good shepherd goes until he finds the lost sheep. This by no means suggests that every lost sheep will be found. Paul says in 1 Corinthians 9:22 (King James Version) *"To the weak became I as weak, that I might gain the weak: I am made all things to all men, that I might by all means save some"*. The goal is to ensure that we give our all, even though in the end we will not get all to be saved.

It is not part of our work description to determine who can or cannot be saved. God desires that all should be saved (2 Peter 3:9). So we must preach the gospel to every creature (Mark 16:16). When a fisher man casts his net into the river to catch fish, some fishes will jump out as he pulls. He knows he will not catch all the fishes in the river, but he does not get discouraged from fishing all together; he knows he will catch some. We must apply this same principle in reaching out to the lost, after all, we are fishers of men. (Matthew 4:19).

So Jesus continued with his response to the elders' denouncement of him. Luke 15:5 (Revised Standard Version) *"And when he has found it, he lays it on his shoulders rejoicing"*. Oh how the thought of it just blesses my heart. When the lost sheep is eventually found, it may be with a broken limb or with some other injury. The sheep is certainly weary from hunger, thirst and from wandering in the harsh elements. Too exhausted to walk the long journey back to the pen, it is lifted and supported by the ever strong shoulders of the shepherd and brought to its place of rest in the shepherd's bosom. What a picture of perfect love; only the Father can set this standard of love for us to follow. Only Jesus could have demonstrated this unconditional love on the cross, laying down his life for his strayed sheep. *For we all like sheep have gone astray; we have turned everyone to his own way; and*

the Lord has laid on him the iniquity of us all.
(Isaiah 53:6 King James Version).

It is clear that what Jesus intended with this parable was to demonstrate the length he would go to save the lost. When the shepherd finds the missing sheep, he carries it on his shoulders with much rejoicing, inviting his friends to share in his joy.

But wait a minute! Now the lost but found sheep is being celebrated like a hero. Why should it have to be carried on the shepherd's shoulders in the first place. Is that supposed to be an incentive? Looks more like good reward for bad behavior. How about some form of punishment? I would suggest that punishment should begin from the moment the sheep is found. How about tying a rope around its neck, albeit not too tightly and then pulling it along so it walks the whole distance back to the pen? At least just to have a taste of what the shepherd went through to find it. How about some kicks at the rear, not to cause injury though, but just enough to cause that shock effect? Just enough to at least provoke honest answers to a few pertinent questions such as; "what were you doing when the shepherd's call came that it was time to go? Did you not notice when the large mass of furry herd walked away from you? Was all the bleating sound from the rest of your kind not noise loud enough for you to hear? So what went wrong?

But our God is not a man, he is nothing like man. He is neither bankrupt of mercy nor lacking in grace. His forgiveness is never in short supply. The stream of his affection flows ever so freely and extravagantly, for he himself is love. Anything short of this attitude neither describes our loving father nor Jesus whom he sent to seek and to save the lost.

Jesus concludes this parable by highlighting an important detail; Luke 15:7 "**Just so, I tell you, there will be more joy in heaven over**

one sinner who repents, than over ninety-
nine righteous persons who need no
repentance" (English Standard Version).
Notice that he does not say there is less
rejoicing over the ninety-nine who do not
need repentance, because the rejoicing
continues over the ones that are safe.
Rejoicing never reduces in the kingdom. "For
the kingdom of God is... righteousness and
peace and joy in the Holy Spirit" Romans
14:17. Contrary to what some people think,
God does not love you less after you are born
again. He is not like some earthly parents
who pay less attention to the older ones as
soon as they have a new baby, no. He
continues to rejoice over you causing you to
experience the heights, depths, length and
breathe of his love. "And I ask him that with
both feet planted firmly on love, you'll be
able to take in with all followers of Jesus the
extravagant dimensions of Christ's love.
Reach out and experience the breadth! Test
its length! Plumb the depths! Rise to the
heights! Live full lives, full in the fullness of

God" Ephesians 3:17-19. The Message Bible. The joy level in the kingdom is never toned down; it only increases. It is rather toned up whenever a sinner repents. Hallelujah! Have you toned up heaven's joy this week? You can do something about it; go win a soul now! Go in search, until...

Chapter 3

Get Under the Furniture, Sweep the Lost Out!

J esus was not willing to let this go easy; the religious leaders had interrupted his beautiful outreach session. Jesus approach to saving the lost was most unconventional; his approval ratings were very low amongst the religious rulers. Once he had lunch with a certain Mr. Simon, a Pharisee. As Jesus sat to eat, a sinner woman who had obviously trailed him to the house went to him and worshipped him breaking her alabaster box of ointment on him. She went on further to wet his feet with her tears and dry them with her hair. As she began kissing his feet, Simon said within himself, *"if he was truly a prophet, he would have known the kind of woman it was that touched him"*. Again, this was an unconventional approach; allowing a sinner woman to touch him. (Luke 7:36-50). It mattered more to them the approach, than it did the act of reaching out to the sinner. They would rather that Jesus had stood at a distance and called out loudly to sinners everywhere to repent. That was the approach at some point in history; in the days of the prophets of old. It is characteristic of the spirit of the law to call out to people from a distance. John 1:17 **"For the law was given by Moses, but grace and truth came by Jesus Christ" (KJV).** Moses stood at a distance and read the laws out to the people. But grace and truth came; in a personal way, and made a move towards us in the person of Jesus Christ. When Jesus came preaching the gospel of the kingdom of God, he presented the kingdom as one that was already at hand, i.e. near you. He commanded his disciples to heal the sick and say to the people *"... the kingdom of God has come near to you". Luke*

10:9. He didn't present the father as being afar off and calling on sinners everywhere to hurriedly repent before he changed his mind. No. God so loved the world that he sent his son to die for the sins of the world. Jesus was the sent one. Not even the scrutiny of his approach by the religious power-house would deter him from his business of saving lives; he had another question for them. He wasn't done just yet:

"Or what woman, having ten silver coins, if she loses one coin, does not light a lamp, sweep the house, and search carefully until she finds it? And when she has found it, calls her friends and neighbours together, saying, 'rejoice with me, for I have found the piece which I lost' Likewise, I say to you, there is joy in the presence of the angels of God over one sinner who repents"

We must be wary of any structure or program that makes us comfortable with sitting down and waiting for sinners to come to us. The woman in Jesus' parable does not sit and do a casual scan of her living room in search of her missing coin. She lights a lamp, gets a broom and sweeps, searching every nook and cranny; she gets under every piece of furniture until she finds her missing coin. The point that is impossible to miss is that the coin was of great value to her.

Speaking about great value, it would take being a shepherd in Jesus day to appreciate why a shepherd would go to such great lengths to find one missing sheep. By the same token, it would take being a woman in Jesus day to appreciate what that coin must have meant to that woman. But for knowledge of the historical background, which tell that the coins were usually part of a woman's dowry; we may not appreciate the fact that they were some of her very prized possessions.

Sinners are God's prized possessions; he will do all to find them.

Jesus was leaving no stone unturned; receiving sinners and eating with them was simply his way of lighting his lamp, taking his broom and sweeping out the entire house. *John 20:21 "... as the father has sent me, I also send you".* We too must rise from the comfort of our organized religious structures; we must no longer sit down and leisurely scan around to see if sinners came for our meetings. Chairs, tables, cupboards, and beds (organized religion) will have to be moved around a bit, and religious people will get uncomfortable. They are the ones who sit on those chairs, too relaxed to go preach the gospel; They dine on the goodness of God and forget to spread that goodness around. They lie in beds of comfort without any sense of urgency to redeem the time and begin laboring in the harvest fields. It is these ones that will get uncomfortable when furniture gets moved around. Moving furniture around, means that we will be employing unconventional ways of reaching out to the lost, much to the disgust of organized religion.

Becoming All Things To All Men!

It was unconventional for Jesus to sit and eat with sinners. Paul put it this way;

"When I am with the Jews, I seem as one of them so that they will listen to the gospel and I can win them to Christ. When I am with the Gentiles who follow Jewish customs and ceremonies I don't argue, even though I don't agree, because I want to help them. When with the heathen I agree with them as much as I can, except of course that I must always do what is right as a Christian. And so, by agreeing, I can win their confidence and help them too. When I am with those whose consciences bother them easily, I don't act as though I know it all and don't say they are foolish; the result is that they are willing to let me help them. Yes, whatever a person is like, I try to find

common ground with him so that he will let me tell him about Christ and let Christ save him. I do this to get the gospel to them and also for the blessing I myself receive when I see them come to Christ" 1 Corinthians 9:20-23. The Living Bible (TLB)

"Go ye into all the world..." (Mark 16:15. King James Version) means going wherever unbelievers are. We must be willing to stay up late and meet them in the night clubs, pubs or beer palours (it is advisable we go in groups, Jesus always sent his disciples out in pairs). We must be willing to meet them in the most "unholy" of places. Becoming all things to all men means that we must be wise enough to camouflage and adapt to different scenarios and circumstances. Finding common ground with sinners does not include compromising our godly values; rather, it involves finding points of agreement in order to gain an entrance into their hearts. It goes beyond just being nice and making friends; we must be very intentional about winning the lost and reaching out as well to weak Christians.

It is time to rise up, shed the weight of religious decorum and do some 'unconventional stuff' to reach the lost. We must now light our lamps, shine light in the darkness, go under the furniture, stick our broom into every corner and sweep sinners out.

Chapter 4

He Loves Even Them...!

In view of the insensitivity of the religious rulers to the intents and purposes of the Father God, Jesus took them on a journey into the heart of the father; a world they had never known. Nothing else compares to the compassionate love of the Father. No one experiences it and remains the same. It is on this same journey that the proceeding chapters take us; for though some may not be hard on others, they certainly are on themselves, not missing any occasion to inflict condemnation on themselves for their shortcomings. Never before had the religious leaders perceived the Father in the manner that Jesus was about to present him. Imagine we are all locked up in a vehicle with the religious leaders of Jesus' day, and Jesus got the wheels; now he's driving us down the father's love road as our tour guide, a road we've never been on before. Fasten your seatbelts, it gets pretty enchanting.

Luke 15:11-32

Vs 11 "... A certain man had two sons" (KJV)
This is the story popularly referred to as 'The Prodigal Son'. This title can be a bit misleading as it puts the spotlight on the younger son, rather than on the father. Whereas it is clear from the opening statement that the focus is on the father. It begins with: "A certain man..." not, "A certain prodigal son". To gain a better understanding of this story, we must keep our focus on the father. The younger son as we shall soon observe in the story is a type of the sinners that Jesus sat and ate with. It is common for sinners to commit sin, just as it is

common for children to misbehave; there's really no news here. Sinners do what sinners do: commit sin. So the goal of Jesus in telling this story was not to give some special revelation or insight into the terribleness of sinners; rather, it was to give insight into the amazing heart of the Father. The heart from which stemmed such compassionate response to an undeserving sinner. That is where the big deal is my friend, that is what made the news in this story; the Father's compassionate response!

Vs 12 "And the younger of them said to his father, Father, give me the share of property that falls to me. And he divided his living between them" (RSV)

The younger son asked for his share of the family inheritance; the father divided his property, and gave to both sons. Yes, he gave to both of them. We have all easily missed this detail in the story, including myself. So you can imagine my surprise when I discovered it was so. There are no insignificant details in scripture, and we shall refer back to this point in a while.

Vs 13 "And not many days later, the younger son gathered all he had and took his, journey into a far country, and there he squandered his property in loose living".

For the Jews in Jesus' day, a far country didn't just mean a country far away from theirs. A far country also meant a place where Gentiles dwelt, which could have been the neighbouring community. The Jews held to this belief because most Gentiles were ungodly people and so they were considered strangers and a distant people. We see this captured in the writings of Paul from a Jewish perspective; remember he was a Jew. Ephesians 2:12-13 *"remember that you were at that time separated from Christ, alienated from the commonwealth of Israel, and strangers to the covenant of promise., having no hope and without God in the world. But now in Christ Jesus, you who once were far off have been brought near in the blood of Christ. For he is our peace, who has made us both one, and has broken down the dividing wall of hostility"*. Here, Paul the Apostle explains clearly that we were strangers and were afar off as unbelieving Gentiles. This was the way Jews saw Gentiles. So indications are that the younger son went to reside amongst Gentiles and so was considered to have gone to a distant land. This thought is further strengthened by the fact that the older brother seemed to know all that the younger brother did while he was away. He said later in verse 30 *"But when this son of yours came, who has devoured your living with harlots..."* Indications are that the far country was a place nearby, dominated by Gentiles, where his escapades could still be known. He wasted his inheritance on riotous living until it was all completely exhausted; his whole future, presently spent.

Vs 14 -16 "And when he had spent everything, a great famine arose in that country, and he began to be in want. So he went and joined himself to one of the citizens of that country, who sent him into his fields to feed swine. And he would gladly have fed on the pods that the swine ate; and no one gave him anything"

Again we see that this was a Gentile settlement rather than a Jewish enclave, because Jews were forbidden to rear swine.

Vs 17 "But when he came to himself he said, 'How many of my father's hired servants have bread enough and to spare, but I perish here with hunger..."

It is important to ensure at this juncture, that the picture so far has been well captured in our minds, and no detail is missed. The story is painted on a Jewish canvass and can only be understood thereupon. The younger of the two sons asked his father for his share of the inheritance; the father divided his belongings between them ensuring that each one got his share. The younger one took all his inheritance and left for a distant land. This had grievous implications in the culture of the day, and even in modern cultures; the boy was in essence saying to his father *'Look sir, I've waited a long time for you to die so I can begin to enjoy my inheritance, but I can't wait any longer. So let me have my share now'.* Hebrews 9:16-17 **"For where a will is involved, the death of the one who made it must first be established. For a will takes effect only at death, since it is not in force as long as the one who made it is still alive"** He was saying to his father in essence; *'I consider you dead in my estimation, so I'll just go ahead and have my share of the inheritance'* This would be the highest insult a son could give his father; and the religious leaders understood this perfectly. The first shocker is that the father obliged; he didn't have to; it was his prerogative. He could have said no! He could have sent the boy away with nothing; the call was his to make.

But then, the father gave; and then, the son left. This again was serious; the boy had in essence completely cut all ties with his father. It was the final nail in the coffin; it was the seal of the insult! On that fateful day, the boy left home, leaving his father with a wounded heart, the father looked on as the distance between them widened. He still remembered clearly the day of his birth; the cry of his second male child tore through the tensions of an expecting household. Shattering the silent worries and unspoken fears, it paved way for a flush of joy and wild excitement. How he rejoiced at being a father of two. Rocking the boy in his arms he imagined only fun times ahead with his cute little prince as they would run around in the yard, cheered upon by the attending servants. All that light suddenly turned dark as that once tender child now turned callous and soulless, continued disappearing into the distance. With all innocence eroded and the limits of rebellion exceeded, he walked off without a moment's glance at the teary eyes of his fainting father. The distance widened, the father sullen, as he watched his boy become a spot in the horizon, and disappear.

According to the custom, it could not be undone; the son could never reverse what he had done, a road of no return. If the religious leaders were truly listening to Jesus story, you can be sure that the expressions on their faces were a mixture of bewilderment and disapproval.

Then famine struck! He was hungry and nobody gave him anything. Just when you thought it couldn't get any worse, he takes it to a new low by joining himself with a pig farmer. That may have no serious implications in our day but for the Jews, it is forbidden till date. Pigs are regarded as unclean in Jewish law. The young man had now fallen to the lowest place possible, rearing pigs and even desiring their food for lunch. To the Jews, nothing could be worse off; he had fallen from grace to abyss.

Let us not forget from where this all started; Jesus was enjoying lunch with a bunch of really bad guys. The Scribes and Pharisees would have none of it. Their disgust was unbridled; "this man receives sinners and eats with them". Jesus responded with a trilogy; the first two were pretty straightforward and easily understood by the religious leaders. But this third one was becoming quite exhaustive, with unpredictable twists. So where was Jesus going with this story? What was he about to illustrate? Did he even have to explain his actions to these insensitive, hard-boiled, compassionless, case-hardened, and self-righteous bigots? Were they even relevant in the scheme of things? Why did he attempt to carry them along? The reason was because; they were the older brother in the story who stayed home; they too deserve the father's love.

Chapter 5

Let Me Clean Up My Mess!

Luke 15:11-31

Vs 17 "But when he came to himself he said 'How many of my father's hired servants have bread enough and to spare, but I perish here with hunger! I will arise and go to my father, and I will say to him, "Father, I have sinned against heaven and before you; I am no longer worthy to be called your son; treat me as one of your hired servants."'

This is where the young man begins to have a

change of heart and turns a new leaf. He realizes that he went too far and that his father must have been so heart broken. Having realized his wrong, he decided on making a U-turn; far from it!

That young man had absolutely no remorse. Jesus never intended to paint that idea in the story. The sinners that Jesus was feasting with, who were exemplified by the young man in the story, were not remorseful sinners. They were current sinners! Had they taken to their knees in regretful soberness, begging for mercy before the master, the religious rulers would have gladly joined in the restoration ceremony. But their lack of penitence was part of the reasons for the frustrations of the religious rulers; how in the world could Jesus be friendly with unrepentant sinners? It was an outright endorsement of their lifestyle.

How often are we awakened to our own sense of holiness when in the midst of unrelenting sinners; the awareness that we are the better, and they are the worse; the awareness that creates a distance rather than bridging the gap? Sadly, this is carnality in its humblest form; pride in the garb of decency. If Christ who is holiness personified did not feel uncomfortable around sinners, then neither should we. It is not a spiritual virtue. If you cannot relate well with sinners, then you probably are not an active soul winner. There are some that will be on your target list for a while; your only chance of winning them for Christ is to wine, dine and be friendly with them. With clarity of purpose, and a healthy consciousness of the Christ life in you, there is no fear of compromising your godly values. The only thing you'll ever have to bother about is the cynicism of religious folks. Jesus dealt with it, so should you.

The young man was not a bit sorry. So what was his spur to go back? It's simple; Hunger! Hear it from the horse's mouth: **"How many of my father's hired servants have bread**

enough and to spare, but I perish here with hunger! I will arise and go to my father…"

That doesn't sound anything like a repentant fellow; the lad simply did not want to die of hunger. Clearly, if he were not hungry, thoughts about his father may never have arisen in his mind. Even hired servants were better served in life than he was; it was time to jump out of the sinking ship. It is called "Crisis Management" Not repentance!

One heartening attribute of God is His tender loving kindness; for him, it really doesn't matter that you now seek him simply because you have problems. He's not going to say: *"Aha! Gotcha! So finally you now acknowledge your need of me! Was wondering how long it would take. So give me one good reason why I should help you?* Rather, He'll receive you just as you are and be gracious to a fault. The Father's love precedes our repentance; his love moves us to repentance. **Romans 2:4 "Or do you think lightly of his abundant**

kindness, patience, and forbearance, not realizing that his kindness is meant to lead you to repentance?" (Twentieth Century New Testament). The economy of salvation is what only God could have accomplished; man only has to receive by faith. The boy's restoration had nothing to do with him. He was not even reaching out for it; he knew by now it was beyond his reach; he cried: *"I am no longer worthy to be called your son"* This was not an attempt to patronize his father. It was a statement of fact, and was sincerely stated. He was content to be something else; a hired servant. Many sinners are hired servants. They do good things around the world, helping the poor, donating millions of dollars to eradicate sickness, aid victims of natural disasters and wars etc. they are all carrying out God's will. God loves humanity and does not want to see them suffer. He has enabled these philanthropists to prosper financially with skill and talent, and he uses them to bring relief to a troubled world. Yet, at best they are hired servants. They are hired to do some work and are paid for it. But sadly, their good deeds cannot save them, and make them sons in the house.

The Pride of Guilt!

VS 18 "I will go to my father, and say to him, "Father, I have sinned against God in heaven and against you. I am no longer good enough to be called your son. Treat me like one of your workers." (Contemporary English Version).

Now isn't this absolutely commendable? When we do wrong we must learn to take responsibility. Experience had taught him that money was hard to come by. Had he realized this earlier, he would not have squandered his share of the inheritance. But now he realized it; it was time to make up for lost glory and resources. So his proposal in essence was; *"I don't want freebies any more, no more handouts; I want to earn whatsoever I get by working with my own hands".* As noble and responsible as this sounds, it is called "The Pride of Guilt". God's response is; "Thanks, but no thanks".

No man can cleanse himself of his sins before the Father; only the blood of Jesus. The only thing that could ever atone for the sins of man was the blood, and that blood price has been paid fully by Jesus Christ. If we could somehow by our self-efforts, right our wrongs, then Christ died in vain. Galatians 2:21 *"I do not frustrate the grace of God: for if righteousness come by the law then Christ is dead in vain".* (KJV). Some people, after doing many bad things in their lives, and even prospered financially by their evil deeds, now attempt to pay for their sins by donating to charities, orphanages and poor people. They think that any good they do will cancel out some of their bad. It doesn't work that way. Let go and let God. He has made a way for your total cleansing; your sins are already forgiven you by the blood of Christ. If you insist on atoning for your sins by your own self-efforts, then you are claiming to be wiser than God. Let go and let God; the blood sacrifice of Christ has appeased God's anger forever. God is no longer angry with you; all you have to do is believe in the sacrifice of Jesus on the cross. Accept that he died for you as punishment for every sin you have ever and could ever commit. Jesus blood has paid in full.

Chapter 6

Then Love Interrupts!

"And he arose and came to his father. But while he was yet at a distance, his father saw him and had compassion, and ran and embraced him and kissed him. And the son said to him, 'Father, I have sinned against heaven and before you; I am no longer worthy to be called your son.' But the father said to his servants, 'Bring quickly the best robe, and put it on him; and put a ring on his hand, and shoes on his feet; and let us eat and make merry; for this my son was dead and is alive again; he was lost and is found.' And they began to

make merry. Luke 15:20 (KJV)

Two hearts in stark contrast; one riddled with condemnation, the other smeared with compassion. One distant heart, headed home, the other racing to shorten the distance; desperate to close the gap. The religious leaders listening to Jesus story could tell that the boy was not repentant; but he sure wanted a way out of his predicament. The best solution he could come up with however was not one that would restore him to sonship. It is important to emphasize that the boy could do nothing about returning to his former position as a son. According to the culture of the day, the moment the son asked the father for his share of the property, received it and walked away, he had in effect irreversibly severed all ties with his father. The will should only have taken effect after the death of the father. So by asking for, receiving and walking away with his share of the property, the younger son implied that his father was already dead in his own estimation. This being the case, the boy had therefore nobody to come back to in repentance to ask to be restored to sonship. This was what inspired the statement *"I am no longer worthy to be called your son..."* The word "worthy" is derived from the Greek word {axios}, it means having the weight of another thing of like value, or, worth as much (Strongs Concordance). In other words, the boy was simply saying; "I no longer have the value of a son, my actions have robbed me of my value as a son. I have no more worth in that regard, I no longer have the weight of a son. I have now lost the essence or substance that make for sonship"

Brothers and sisters, these were no mere words spoken to gain sympathy; they were the conclusions of a heart filled with fatal hopelessness; words of total surrender to a horrendous reality. He had no more rights or privileges, no more claims to make. No man in this state could ever truly help himself. He could not cry or beg his way back to sonship;

nothing that came from him could have qualified him to become a son again. He had settled for the role of hired servant. The boy could not have demanded it; he could only receive it, if the father offered it.

A single thread runs through the three stories; it was the shepherd who went after the lost sheep, not the other way around. If we ever stray away from God, it is God who comes looking for us, and not us looking for him. It was the woman who searched to find her missing coin, and not the other way around. If we get so lost in sin and binding addictions, it is not us who go back searching for God, it is God who comes searching until He finds us out. In this last parable, just like the sheep could not go in search for the shepherd, and the coin could not go find the woman, so the boy had no capacity to go ask for sonship. It was way beyond him now. In that regard, he had no more fight left in him. What we are about to witness is such graciousness as could only have been given by the father.

It wasn't a son coming back home, No! It was a total stranger seeking a job as a hired servant. He had just come from feeding pigs. So he "looked pig" and "smelt pig".

The boy makes a move for the role of a hired servant, the father makes his move to restore him to sonship.

Everyday since the boy left, the father's heart never stopped hoping, never stopped desiring to see the boy return. Each day he would go out to the road where his loved one departed, anticipating; "maybe today my boy will return". And then one day, that spot resurfaced, increasing in size, and gradually developing into what looked like his boy. While still a great way off, the father recognized him and ran to him and kissed him. It's amazing that the father still recognized him in his state. Even when we think we're too far gone for God to reach, God never relaxes his hold on us. Even when we no longer recognize ourselves, God still recognizes us. It is while we were yet sinners that Christ died for us.

The father ran towards the boy; this was no mean gesture, it bears describing. In the culture of the day, rich men such as these were decked in flowing robes. I imagine that he held up his robe on both sides to give his legs enough room to run. Oh what a sight that must have been; I imagine people wondering and asking "what troubles him this much? We have never before seen him agitated. What makes today different? Who is he running towards? The father embraces him and showers him with kisses; and then the boy begins to act out all he has premeditated: *...I have sinned against heaven and in thy sight, and am no more worthy to be called your son..."* At this point the father cuts him short; love interrupts!

How have we managed to settle with the idea

that the father is very particular about how well we cry for forgiveness? How did we come to believe that God only hears us after we have passionately cried bitter tears of sorrow for repentance? Our attempt to put on modern day sackcloth ridicules the essence of the cross of Christ. Forgiveness is not a reward for our bitter tears; it is a gift of God's grace. And we are to receive it by faith. It is not required that we beat ourselves so hard in order to show God that we are truly sorry. We should not have more faith in our sorrowing than in the cross of Christ. In the New Testament, a broken and a contrite heart is one that believes the foolish message of the cross. It is one that looks solely to the blood sacrifice of Jesus on the cross as its redemption. Nothing more, nothing less. God has determined the means by which forgiveness is received; faith in the appeasement sacrifice of Christ. **"I do not frustrate the grace of God: for if righteousness come by the law, then Christ is dead in vain". Galatians 2:21** , (KJV)

Chapter 7

Now this is Prodigal!

"**B**ut the father said to his servants, bring forth the best robe and put it on him; and put a ring on his hand, and shoes on his feet: and bring in the fatted calf, and kill it and let us eat and be merry: For this my son was dead, and is alive again; he was lost and is found. And they began to be merry". Luke 15:22-23 (KJV)

A story was told about Alexander the Great, when he took a walk with one of his generals, admiring his vast empire. He met a poor beggar who asked of him some alms.

Alexander **promptly** gave him some gold coins. Amazed, the general asked him why he chose to give the beggar gold coins instead of copper. "he's just a beggar" the general said; Alexander replied "Copper coins suit the beggar, but gold coins suit my giving"

'And my God shall supply all your needs according to his riches in glory by Christ Jesus' Philippians 4:19. (KJV). This means that God does not meet our needs according to our need; he meets our needs according to his abundance. It suits his giving to give us much more than we require. The bible describes God as extravagant in his display of love. We must not restrict him to the confines of our little human minds. Everything God does is mega. It's who He is.

Ephesians 1:7 **"In him we have redemption through his blood, the forgiveness of sins according to the riches of his grace"**. (KJV). Again we see that he forgave us, not according to the degree of our sins, but according to the riches of his grace. This is the mental picture we must have of God.

Now you understand why Jesus would present the father in his story as extravagant, He was depicting God. We must remember that the focus of Jesus story was not on the misbehavior of the son but on the loving heart of the father. The great lengths that Jesus went in describing the boy's sins were not to magnify them or to do a special documentary on sin; No. Rather, He did it to cast the exceeding riches of God's grace against the background of heinous sin. He did it to reveal the great extent God is willing and able to go for even one lost soul.

So after capturing the son's rebellion, the camera now focuses on the father and zooms in on his response; which truly is not reactionary, but in continuance of a love process that the boy walked out of. Yes, God is not reactive, but proactive. Nothing takes God unawares! Romans 11:34-35 **"and who**

could ever offer to the Lord enough to
induce him to act?" **(The Living Bible)**. God
is the initiator. No man ever came to God in
and of himself; he had to have been
responding to God's pull. Jesus put it this
way **"No man can come to me except the
Father which hath sent me draw him..."**
John 6:44. If ever there was anything we did
to please God, it was Him all the while **"...at
work in us both to will and to do of his good
pleasure" Philippians 2:13.**

In no particular order, the three instructions
the father gave were a direct negation of the
three-part solution the boy had thought up:

**"I have sinned against heaven and against
you" - "Bring forth the best robe and put it
on him"**

**"I am no longer worthy to be called your
son" - "Put shoes on his feet"**

"Take me as one of your hired servants" -

"Put a ring on his hand"

The implications are interesting; for the first one, it was easy for any Jew to understand why the father would ask that a new robe be given the son. The robe signifies righteousness. The term "robe of righteousness" was of common usage in Israel. Isaiah 61:10 **"I will greatly rejoice in the Lord, my soul shall be joyful in my God; for he hath clothed me with the garments of salvation, he hath covered me with the robe of righteousness..."** When the boy said "I have sinned against heaven and before you, he was saying **"I have soiled my robe"**. The father's matching response was: **"Bring forth the best robe and put it on him"**.

The word "best" is the Greek word {protos}. It means more than just the best in the collection; it means first of its kind, most important of all and the highest in rank. So the father didn't just send for another robe, there was a specific one he asked for. And he said "**...put it on him**". This phrase is one word in the Greek. It was also used in Galatians 3:27 **"For as many of you as have been baptized into Christ have 'put on' Christ"**. It is the Greek word {Enduo}, and it literally means {to sink into a clothing, to put it on so that you are completely covered in it.

This robe is none other than Christ himself who has become our righteousness. 1 Corinthians 1:30 **"But of him are ye in Christ Jesus who of God is made unto us...righteousness..."**. This righteousness is the first of its kind. It is superior to the righteousness of the law. It is the most important of all and the highest in rank and quality. Jesus is not more righteous than the believer; it is his very righteousness that we have because we have "put on Christ". He is our righteousness. This is the only righteousness that God approves of; He calls it his own righteousness. There is the righteousness of man, and there is the righteousness of God. The righteousness of man is man's attempt to earn salvation by his good works. The righteousness of God is by faith in Christ Jesus alone. Hallelujah!

Romans 10:3-4. **"for they being ignorant of God's righteousness, and going about to establish their own righteousness, have not submitted themselves unto the righteousness of God. For Christ is the end of the law for righteousness to everyone that believes"**. This is the reason why the father did not ask the boy to do anything to make up for his sins; he could never have righted his wrong. It was solely up to his father to restore to him his rights as a son. We cannot do anything about our sins, only God can cleanse and restore us to sonship.

Did you notice that the boy did not ask for forgiveness before he was forgiven? Neither did he confess the exact sin or sins he committed while he was away. This should come as no surprise at all as Jesus himself, once and again, forgave people who did not ask for it. On one occasion, Jesus was teaching in a house. Four men brought in their friend on a stretcher. Jesus looked at the man on the stretcher and said to him; **"Cheer up, son. I forgive your sins. Some religion scholars whispered, "why, that's blasphemy"** Matthew 9:3. (Message Bible). On yet another occasion, Jesus was eating in the house of a Pharisee named Simon. A woman who was a known sinner came in to see Jesus. Without saying a word, she broke her alabaster box of fragrant ointment and poured it on Jesus. Then she began wetting his feet with her tears and drying them with her hair; and did not stop kissing his feet. In the end Jesus said to Simon, who was already angry that Jesus would allow a sinner touch him in the first place; **"So I'm telling you that her sins, as many as they are, have been forgiven, and that's why she has shown such great love. But the one to whom little is forgiven loves little".** Luke 7:47 (International Standard Version. ISV). Again here, there is no record that she asked for her sins to be forgiven. It seems to me that Jesus went around forgiving sins because he knew he would pay for them all later with his own blood. It is the knowledge and the consciousness of the total forgiveness of our sins, past, present and future, that produces such great love and passion for God in our hearts. If people can get to realize that God loves them and has forgiven them of all their sins, they will love God better. 1 John 4:19 says **"We love him, because he first loved us"**. (KJV). So our love for God is in response to his love for us. Hear it from Jesus' own mouth in Luke 7:47 from the Easy English Translation; **"So I tell you this. This woman has done many bad things. But I have forgiven them. She loves me a lot, because I have forgiven her a lot. If I only forgive a little, a person only loves me a little"**

In the New Testament, forgiveness of sins is always presented as what God has accomplished for us in the past tense, and as something that we now have in the present tense. Very importantly, it is presented as an act of God's grace rather than as a reward for our asking for it. Ephesians 1:7 **"In him we have redemption through his blood and the forgiveness of sins according to the riches of His grace"**. (Modern English Version). Here we see that forgiveness of sins is what we now have in the present. Ephesians 4:32 **"And be ye kind one to another, tenderhearted, forgiving one another, even as God for Christ's sake hath forgiven you"**. (KJV). Here we see the forgiveness of our sins as what God has done in the past. Colossians 3:13 **"Forbearing one another, and forgiving one another, if any man have a quarrel against any: even as Christ forgave you, so also do ye"**. (KJV). Again in this scripture we see our forgiveness in the past tense. In fact, we are told to forgive others because we have been forgiven. It means that God teaches us to forgive by his own example of forgiveness. He first forgives us then says to us, "do likewise"

Acts 13:38-39 **"Be it known unto you therefore men and brethren that through this man is preached unto you the forgiveness of sins: and by him all that believe are justified from all things from which ye could not be justified by the laws of Moses"**. (KJV). This is the message that we preach; the total forgiveness of sins. past, present and future. But to appropriate its benefits in your life you must believe it. It says **"...all who believe are justified from all things..."** To be justified means to be declared innocent, not guilty, and righteous. But you must first believe the message. Isaiah 53:1 says, **"Who has believed our report..."** 1 John 4:16 says **"And we have known and believed the love that God hath to us. God is love..."** It is faith in this total forgiveness of sins that delivers to us the free gift of righteousness. Yes, righteousness is a gift. Romans 5:17-18 **"For if by one man's offence death reigned by one; much more they which receive abundance of grace and of the GIFT OF RIGHTEOUSNESS shall reign in life by**

one, Jesus Christ. Therefore, as by the offence of one judgement came upon all men to condemnation; even so by the righteousness of one the free gift came upon all men unto justification of life".

This righteousness that comes by Christ does not diminish in quality or value. Even when we sin as believers, it is not the least affected.

The believer in Christ does not enjoy sin; he does not want to sin because he has crucified the flesh with its passions. (Galatians 5:24). But sometimes he may fall into sin by yielding to the promptings of the flesh, or he may even relapse into carnality like the Corinthian church. Yet, his righteousness is intact because the righteousness he has received does not expire or reduce in quality. It is sin proof! Sin cannot soil it!

This is by no means a license to sin. No. It's like owning an expensive water resistant phone. That does not encourage you to throw your phone into every pool of water you find. That's not the purpose for the phone. But in case it does fall into water, you can be sure that it will not be damaged. It's the same thing; the purpose for a sin-proof righteousness is not to encourage the believer to begin living in sin. It is so that if he sins, his righteousness is not diminished in any form. The message of grace does not liberate you to sin; rather, it liberates you from sin.

The second thing the boy cried was; **"I am no longer worthy to be called your son"**. The father's matching response was; **"Put shoes on his feet"**. The significance of this response is only appreciated when we see that slaves in their day did not wear shoes. It was only for sons. The boy had returned like a slave; he certainly looked like one. He had no shoes on his feet. The boy cried "I no longer have the value of a son; I am not worth more than a slave now" The father responded; "I will not leave you in the fashion of a slave, barefooted; I will not allow you run around looking like one". Then to the servants he said; "Put shoes on his feet". Here the father demonstrates to him that he is still a son; only the father could have done this.

Sonship in the New Testament is not something that you grow into. It is a position; a placement in Christ. There is a concept in ancient Greek culture known as "The Placement of Sons" It is the Greek word {uihothesia}. The King James Version translates it as "ADOPTION" or "ADOPTION OF SONS". This concept is much unlike what it means in the English language. Merriam Webster defines the word "adopt" as; "to take a child of other parents legally as your own child". Conversely, adoption in ancient Greek culture was the act of a father conferring the status of mature sonship upon his on biological male child. It meant that the child had come of age and had displayed sound judgement in the execution of his duties as assigned by his father. A ceremony was held publicly to that effect, where the father would announce to all present that he had implicit confidence in his son; and that his son could now stand in for him as regards his business affairs and dealings. From that moment on, whatever the son did or said was as weighty as when the father did or said same. This was what happened with Jesus at his baptism in the river Jordan. God's voice came from heaven at the baptism saying; "...this is my beloved Son, in whom I am well pleased". (Matthew 3:17) KJV. After that endorsement by God the Father, Jesus went forth representing the Father in all things. He boldly declared that anyone who did not honour him was dishonouring the father who sent him. John 5:22-23; **"For the Father judgeth no man, but hath committed all judgement unto the son. That all men should honour the son, even as they honour the Father. He that honoureth not the son honoureth not the father which hath sent him".** KJV.

In the New Testament though, I said earlier

that sonship is not what you grow into; rather it is a position in Christ. This is true. While we will need to grow into fully acknowledging our sonship, we do not grow into sonship. We are as much sons now as we will ever be. In Galatians, Paul talks about our being children in the past tense, which is in reference to being under the laws of Moses. You give rules and regulations to children in order to regulate their conduct. Then he goes further to refer to us as mature sons in the present tense. Galatians 4:3-7; **"Even so we when we were children, were in bondage under the elements of the world: But when the fullness of time was come, God sent forth his son, made of a woman, made under the law, to redeem them that were under the law, that we might receive the adoption of sons. And because ye are sons, God hath sent forth the Spirit of his Son into your hearts crying, Abba, Father. Wherefore thou art no more a servant, but a son; and if a son, then an heir of God through Christ"**. Notice that verse five says; **"...that we might receive**

the adoption of sons..." It does not say we should grow into it. We have received it. It is not grown into, it is received. Romans 8:15 **"For ye have not received the spirit of bondage again to fear; but ye have received the Spirit of adoption, whereby we cry, Abba, Father".** KJV. This means that we have received the Spirit that confers mature sonship upon us.

Aside the wonderful privilege of having to stand in for the Father, this conferment of sonship also means that you are a bonafide heir and therefore have full rights to your father's inheritance. It also means that you have access to all that your father owns; he mobilizes you with his resources as you take on responsibilities on his behalf. Galatians 4:7; **"And if you are a child, you're also an heir, with complete access to the inheritance"** (Message Bible).

The implication of the father calling for shoes to be put on the younger son's feet was that the boy's rights had been fully restored, as well as access to all his father had. It also meant that the boy could now take up responsibilities on behalf of his father and would be received with the same honour.

The third cry in the boy's heart was; **"Take me as one of your hired servants"**. But the father interrupted him before he could give voice to it; and replied; **"Put a ring in his hand"**. This ring was more than just a piece of jewelry worn on the finger to make a fashion statement. It was a signet ring used mostly by people with clout and affluence. It had a flat surface with their signature imprinted on it. Whenever they went shopping, they were only required to make an imprint on wax already provided by the shop owner. This was done in order to avoid carrying loads of money around; they were metal currencies unlike our paper currencies today; it would be very inconvenient to carry them about in large quantities. Wearing a signet ring was much like carrying a cheque book or a master card around. Having made the imprint on the substance of wax, the bearer only had to take as much as he wanted from the shop, and then the trader would go to the wealthy man's house at the end of the month, or on an agreed date, and pick the money up himself. It also meant that whoever bore that ring could walk into a shop and pick whatsoever he wanted, and it would be charged to the account of the owner of the ring. As long as an imprint was made on the substance of wax, the signature was undeniable as everyone who owned one of such rings had their unique signature on it.

The father was saying to the boy in essence; "You may no longer have a reputation with people around here. Though I did not expose your sins to the world but some are definitely aware of all that transpired; they may not want to do business with you ever again. But here, take this ring. It's a blank cheque with absolutely no limits on it. You can get as much as you want, whenever you want, no questions asked. If they refuse to do business with you, all you have to do is make that imprint. On my authority, nobody can refuse you".

Having his father's ring on his finger represents for us the wonderful name of Jesus. It is in his name that we cast out demons, heal the sick, raise the dead and walk in victory over Satan. We have no authority in and of ourselves against Satan and his attacks. We have no rights in and of ourselves to enjoy God's blessings in our lives. But God has given us a name whereby we may exercise authority against Satan; and by that same name, we receive whatsoever we ask. John 16:23-24 **"And in that day ye shall ask me nothing. Verily, verily, I say unto you whatsoever ye shall ask the father in my name he will give it you. Hitherto have ye asked nothing in my name: ask, and ye shall receive that your joy may be full".** "In my name" actually means; "In my stead". When we use the name of Jesus, we are actually speaking as him. This is a statement of finality; "whatsoever you ask in that name you will receive". There are no uncertainties surrounding these verses; there are no grey areas. It means that our rights and privileges as sons have been fully restored. We make demands as sons and expect answers. He has given us the right to be confident in asking; our sins have been forgiven and so we do not come before God beggarly and apologetic. No. we are sons, not slaves. Hallelujah! It is not humility to come before God with a sense of inferiority or unworthiness. We have ceased to be strangers before him; we are sons. God does not want us feeling sad and dejected; He wants our joy to be full. He says to ask that we might receive, that our joy might be full. The kingdom of God is **"...righteousness, peace and joy in the Holy Spirit"** Romans 14:17. There must always be rejoicing in God's house. His sons are now home.

The father promptly orders that the fatted

calf be slaughtered and that a huge feast began in commemoration of the coming back of a wayward son. And they began to be merry. What an irony!

The father told his servants to go get him the best robe, shoes for his feet and a ring. While we have already studied the significance of these three items, there is yet something we may not have observed; the father did not wait for them to get home before giving these orders; they were still a great way off. The reason was this; the father was simply saying to his son, "I am not interested in exposing your sins for everyone to know. You left this house looking like royalty, I'll not wait for you to get close enough for people to recognize you in your shame. Here, put on these new change of clothes, your past is safe with me". So bad was this boy's sin that according to the culture of the day, upon the boy receiving his share of the inheritance from his father, a meeting should have been called for where the father would announce to the community what his son had done, and that the boy had in effect been permanently cut off from him. It was the highest offence a son could commit in those days. Yet the father chose to cover his sins and the resulting shame.

God never seeks to expose our sins; rather he has forgiven them and remembers them no more. (Hebrews 8:12). When Jesus was invited to have lunch at the house of Simon the Pharisee. During lunch, a sinner lady walked in, whose track record of sin in the city was known to not just a few. Those around who knew her murmured amongst themselves and said; "If truly he was a prophet of God he would have known the kind of woman it was that touched him" So they presumed that prophetic ministry was to expose the sin in people. But love covers a multitude of sin. 1 Peter 4:8.

Giving the boy new shoes was the main act of reinstating the boy to sonship. Only sons wore shoes; slaves went barefooted. In that singular act, the boy had been restored to the full privileges of sonship. John 1:12 **"But as many as received him, to them gave he the right to become children of God, even to them that believe on his name"** There is a boldness that comes with this; now we can call God "Daddy" and not just "God". The Holy Spirit that we have received is also called the "Spirit of Sonship"; he banishes fear from our lives and gives us the boldness to call God "Daddy" Romans 8:15-16 **"And you did not receive the spirit of religious duty leading you back into the fear of never being good enough. But you have received the spirit of full acceptance, enfolding you into the family of God. And you will never feel orphaned, for as he rises up within us, our spirits join him in saying the words of tender affection, 'beloved Father!' For the Holy Spirit makes God's fatherhood real to us as he whispers into our innermost being, 'you are God's beloved children' (The Passion Translation).** Easy English

Translation Vs 15; **"Because the Spirit that God has given to you does not make you like slaves again. He does not make you slaves which cannot stop being afraid. Instead, the Spirit that God has given to you causes you to become God's children. He makes us able to shout to God: 'you are my Father'**

The word "servant" was used severally in the story; but in the original Hebrew text, it is used in three different forms showing three different kinds of servants:

{Pais}: This was the regular servant or attendant that served in the house. It was this kind of servant that the older brother called.

{Misthios}: This is a hired servant. These don't stay in the house, they are called upon only to do some specific work for which they are paid and they leave. Even they had enough to eat and to spare. The father was very generous to them as well.

{Doulous}: These are called bond slaves who become forever bonded to their masters of their own free will. They have given themselves up for their master's will and are fully devoted to him to the total disregard of their personal interest. It was this set of servants that the father called to bring the change of clothes, shoes and the ring for his son. They were close to the father and attended to him alone. He could trust only them to keep his son's past a secret.

This is how God expects us to be as believers in Christ Jesus; to willingly sell out to Christ completely to do his will and preach the gospel in its simplicity without fear or favour. Paul referred to himself severally as a bond servant of Jesus Christ. In Galatians 1:10 he said; **"...or do I seek to please men? For if I yet please men I should not be the servant (doulous) of Christ."**

The feast that the father organized was much

more than just celebratory; it marked also what was known to the Jews as covenant meal. It was a meal of acceptance or admittance; a meal to receive you into the family fold. This was the reason the older son refused to partake of the feast because in doing so he would be accepting the boy as family. He understood that by throwing a feast the father had received the boy back into the family, and that his rights as a son had been fully restored. So he calls the boy his father's son but not his brother. Hear him for yourself; **"But as soon as this thy son was come..."** (Luke 15:30). He didn't say; "when my brother came back..." he said; "when your son came back". He knew that his father had partaken of the covenant meal of acceptance; but he didn't want to receive his brother back. Jesus said in John 6:56 **"He that eateth my flesh and drinketh my blood, dwelleth in me and I in him"** This happens the moment we believe in Jesus. We are said to have eaten his flesh and drank his blood. In John 6:35 Jesus said; **"...I am the bread of life:**

he that cometh to me shall never hunger; and he that believeth on me shall never thirst." The communion table that we partake of is a demonstration of the covenant meal of acceptance that we partook of and now we have been accepted in the beloved.

Something commendable about the younger son is that he at least knew he had a right to an inheritance, and so dared to ask for it. The older brother didn't seem to realize it and so did not take advantage of it. Luke 15:12 **"And the younger of them said to his father, Father give me the portion of goods that falleth to me. And he divided unto them his living. And not many days after the younger son gathered all together and took his journey into a far country, and there wasted his substance on riotous living."** Notice the emphasis; the boy asked for "his share" of the inheritance. And then the next verse says he wasted "his substance…". It was his and the boy knew it. But compare this with the older brother's remarks; Luke 15:29-30 **"…Lo these**

many years do I serve thee, neither transgressed I at any time thy commandment: and yet thou never gavest me a kid...But as soon as this thy son was come, which hath devoured thy living with harlots, thou hast killed for him the fatted calf" Notice the older brother didn't have any sense of inheritance. First, he accused the father of never giving him even as little as a kid; even though the father had giving them all that he had. He had divided all his living for both sons. Next, he denies that his younger brother ever had any inheritance when he states; "...which hath devoured thy living with harlots...". In other words he still considered the inheritance to be his Father's rather than belonging to both him and his brother. Don't forget though that the father had divided all his belongings to the both of them. The younger one knew this and took his but he didn't take anything. The only problem was the younger son left the presence of his father.

Nothing God gives us should take us away from him. But being in the house should also not stop us from taking as much as we need. Our father is inexhaustible; **He anoints our heads with oil; our cups run over. He has brought us into our wealthy place** (Psalms 23:5; 66:12). The words "run over" and "wealthy place" in the scriptures above are the same Hebrew word {revayah}. It literally means "saturation". That means to overflow or to pour over. That's where God has brought us to in Christ Jesus. Hallellujah! No believer ever needs to suffer lack. When we meet believers who don't understand these truths, we should teach them. And also, we can be answers to their prayers by giving to meet their needs.

Merriam Webster dictionary defines the word prodigal as [carelessly and foolishly spending money, time etc; lavish, reckless]. I say the father was reckless when he ran, closing the distance between him and his 'former son'. I say he was reckless when he fell on his neck and showered him with kisses. I say he was reckless when he gave him a new robe and shoes restoring him to sonship. I say he was careless and doubly reckless when he put a ring; a blank cheque on the hands of a recently proven squanderer of resources. I say he was lavish and inconsiderately careless when he ordered that the fatted calf, the same fatted calf that the older son had been working tirelessly to raise, be killed to provide meat for a lavish celebration that was completely uncalled for. Or was it?

If we would ever conceive of that boy as prodigal, I dare say that the father was several times more prodigal.

Chapter 8

The Offence of Decent Rebels

ow his elder son was in the field: and when he came and drew nigh to the house, he heard music and dancing. And he called one of the servants and asked what these things meant. And he unto him, thy brother is come, and thy father hath killed the fatted calf, because he had received him safe and sound. And he was angry and would not go in: therefore, came his father out, and entreated him. And he answering said to his father, lo these many years do I serve thee, neither transgressed I at any time thy commandment: and yet thou never gavest me a kid that I might make merry with my friends: But as soon as this thy son was come, which hath devoured thy living with harlots, thou hast killed for him the fatted calf. And he said unto him, son, thou art ever with me, and all that I have is thine. It was meet that we should make merry, and be glad: for this thy brother was dead, and is alive again; and was lost and is found' Luke 15:25-32 (KJV)

He got back home with his tools in his hands from a very long day in the bush. He craved for the rest he so badly needed; and deserved. Only three things were on his mind; dinner, a warm bath and a good sleep. He was the decent of the two boys, loyal, faithful to his work and level headed unlike his younger brother. Though dissatisfied with his father's repressed show of love and approval, in spite of his undivided commitment, he never complained nor showed it. For him, this day was much like several others before it;

returning home from the family farm exhausted, he was shutting down for the day. From the distance he heard what would sound like singing and dancing. His conservative mind would not conceive of the possibility that the noise was coming from his house. Nothing prepared him for what he was soon to see. The closer he got, the more he confirmed it.

He had always known his father could be spontaneous. There was always joy around him, even when it was uncalled for. His presence commanded it, his smile exuded it. But this time, things felt strangely different. He stood at the gate and observed; then noticed, beautifully decorated buffet tables positioned at strategic points. Laid on them were delightful and exquisite Jewish cuisine, well coursed out. The aroma of lentil stew prepared with onion, garlic and leeks graced the atmosphere; it was impossible to miss. Quail red stew, and Porridge in beautiful flowery vessels with inscriptions from the

Torah on the sides were neatly arranged.
There were various shapes and sizes of *lehem*,
freshly baked from barley and wheat flour
covered with light napkins to shield them
from the elements. Freshly plucked grapes,
figs, pomegranates, dates, and *tapuah*; all had
their fair share of prominence on the menu;
fruits good for food, pleasant to the eyes,
were also included in the menu. Servants
well dressed for the occasion, carrying food
trays about, treated guests of varying strata to
flavoured steak roast on stakes. Assorted
juices from the grapes and wines from the
vines were borne in jugs ready to be drunk. So
much activity all around, with Abrahamic
music and dance blaring through the
neighbourhood, served to evoke an
obnoxious look on his face as he wondered
what all this meant.

Finally, as he got a grip on himself, he called
one of the servants and asked: "what is the
meaning of all this music and dancing here?"
The servant answered; "your brother is back,

and your father had killed the fatted calf because he had received him safe and sound". In a surge of anger, he turned around, insisting that he would not enter. He had had enough of his Father's extreme benevolence; his mercy priorities were misplaced. It was time for some straight talk with his father; someone had to call him to order.

The excited father came running out to the gate; the excess foliage of his robe in both hands, making his way to his older son. Cutting through his father's entreaties to join in the celebration, with harsh words conveying his heart, it was crystal; all along, the father had two lost sons.

"I have served you faithfully, and never for once disobeyed your instruction. Yet you never gave me even a kid to celebrate with my friends. But when that wayward son of yours returns; you reward him for his rebellion. Where is your sense of fairness

Dad? Have I not done enough to earn even a little of your love? I deserve more than I'm getting?"

My thoughts - If with my brother's blessing comes the realization for me that I am not blessed, then something is wrong.

I am amazed at how the love of the father soothes one and wounds another. Why does she have a better marriage? Why does he have a better job? Why are their children doing better than ours? Why does he have a larger congregation than I do? Someone rightly said; if God blesses your neighbour, get excited and rejoice with them, because God is in your neighbourhood. He will soon get to you.

In Luke 7:11-23, the story is told of how Jesus raised a young boy from the dead; the only son of a widow. Joy filled the whole city as news of the miracle quickly diffused around it. The disciples of John the Baptist, who was now in prison for preaching against the sins of King Herod, hurried to tell him about it. John's response was cold. **"And John calling unto him two of his disciples sent them to Jesus saying Art thou he that should come or look we for another?" (verse 19).** They got to Jesus and informed him of John's skepticism. Jesus responded with more graciousness; he called every sick person he could find around and healed them all in the presence of John's disciples. Then turning to them he said; **"...Go your way and tell John the things ye have seen and heard; how that the blind see, the lame walk, the lepers are cleansed, the deaf hear, the dead are raised, to the poor the gospel is preached. And blessed is he, whosoever is not offended in me".** Wait a minute! Could John actually be offended in Christ? What went wrong? Let's not forget who John the Baptist was; first he was a close relative of Jesus. Mary and Elizabeth, Jesus and John's mothers were cousins. The original translation says they were related by blood, no clarity on the specific kind of relationship. So they may have been closer than cousins. The bottom line is that Jesus and John were closely related. Also, it is very possible that Jesus and John grew up together in the same neighbourhood, and that they were playmates; John was six months older than Jesus as Mary took in when Elizabeth was six months pregnant. Most importantly is the fact that John the Baptist was the forerunner to Jesus. He prepared the way for his coming and eventually announced him to Israel; **"...behold the lamb of God, which taketh away the sin of the world"**. (John 1:29).

If Jesus' closing remark to John's disciples was anything to go by, then it means that at some point, offence had made its way into John's heart. John no doubt had a fantastic resumé as far as doing God's will was concerned; and what is clear is that it was while he was in prison that offence was ever mentioned in connection with John the Baptist. Could it be that he had developed a sense of entitlement as regards God's intervention in his affairs? He probably was at that point where he felt he had earned the right to be delivered from prison by some supernatural means. And if truly Jesus was doing all these miracles for people, then he ought to have been one of the earliest beneficiaries. Notice it was on the occasion of hearing about the miracle of Jesus raising the dead that he sent his disciples to go and ask Jesus if he was truly the Messiah, or if they were to look elsewhere. Offence usually results from an entitlement mentality; it is that feeling that you have paid your dues and therefore have the right to expect a certain output from life or from God. John no doubt must have felt this way. It is called dependence on self-efforts.

Jesus responded by doing more miracles and sent John a solemn rebuke; "blessed is he who is not offended in me". Simply put; "John, do not make me your problem". You must settle it in your heart that God is a good God and that He can never be at fault. If there is a problem, it is never with God. Many, get offended at God because they did not receive a miracle from God. They get offended at Him for failed expectations, a tragedy of some sort, or for some circumstances they can't explain. But if we would just take the time and be open-minded, God will show us areas we would need to make some adjustments, as well as wisdom for the way out of our predicaments.

The older brother was sure that his anger was justified; further aggravated at the thought that his younger brother who was most undeserving, received such undue benevolence. But did he forget? Or had he never realized that all that was left of the inheritance was now his? **Vs 12 "And the younger of them said to his father, Father, give me the share of property that falls to me. And he divided his living <u>between them</u>" (RSV).** How did he not realize this? In this soil is buried the root cause of the offence of decent rebels; it is their insistence on earning by self-efforts what has been freely given by grace. In all their commitment, they have no real love for the father; they seek an occasion to boast in their efforts. The older brother cried; "you have not given me a kid that I might celebrate with my friends" That was the goal; not a celebration with the father, but with his friends. When the younger son returned, the celebration was with the father, not with his friends. Philippians 3:1,3; 4:4 **"Finally my brethren, rejoice in the Lord... For we are the circumcision, who worship God in the spirit, and rejoice in Christ Jesus, and have no confidence in the flesh... Rejoice in the Lord always: and again I say, Rejoice"**

We rejoice in the God of our salvation for the great love with which he has loved us. We celebrate our victory in Christ, not the results of our self-efforts. It is a popular saying that heaven helps those who help themselves. Aside the fact that this is not found anywhere in scripture, the truth is that heaven does not help those who can help themselves. If you can help yourself, you don't need heaven's help. It is only all who labour and are heavy laden that he calls unto and gives help. (Matthew 11:28). Quit working in your own strength; receive the benefits of Christ's finished works. Then let your boast and rejoicing be in Christ alone.

Another thing that depending on your self-efforts does is that it produces in you a sense of unworthiness. You always feel you have not done enough that's why you're not getting the desired results. That feeling that God is not very pleased with you and so is refusing to bless you is nothing short of condemnation. It is not of God. God never gives his children a sense of unworthiness. E.W Kenyon said that righteousness is the ability to stand before God without any sense of guilt or inferiority. God is your father, and you are complete in Christ. **"There is therefore now no condemnation to them that are in Christ Jesus"** (Romans 8:1). Reject those feelings of inadequacy; of never being good enough. It is not your works that count but Jesus work on the cross. The moment you believe in Jesus, you cease from you own labour and enter into rest. (Hebrews 4:10). God now deals with you on the basis of what Christ has done. He blesses you not because of what you've done or not done, but because of what Christ has done. So when next you have a need, don't look to your performance, look to the cross of Christ; therein lies your qualification for any blessing. Halleluyah!

The older brother wanted an occasion to show off to his friends; he had been waiting to get a kid from his father so he could go tell his friends how much he had worked to get it. But all the while he was actually labouring for what had been freely given. He could have as well taken the fatted calf and killed it for barbecue, because all that was left was his anyway. Insisting on self-efforts is choosing to forfeit your inheritance. The inheritance is yours by right of birth; you don't labour for your inheritance.

When a son receives inheritance from his father, what people see are the greatness and excellence of his father. God wants the world to see his glory in us. Depending on our self-efforts glorifies us; receiving God's gifts of grace glorifies Him. Many are frustrated for trusting in their own wisdom. Rest in his grace and enjoy God's best. Halleluyah!

The older son comes back, protests and receives a rebuke. Now, the bad guy looks like the good guy, and the good guy looks like the bad one. Celebrations continue!

Chapter 9

He Has Killed for You

In this final chapter, I seek to paint a clear picture in your mind and heart. The older brother made a remarkable accusation against his father; **"...thou hast killed for him the fatted calf"** (Luke 15:30). God can never, and will never again be angry with the one who has put faith in Jesus. Why? Because He killed for you. It means that though God was angry with you, he found a willing vessel where he channeled all that anger towards. Isaiah 54:8-9 **"I hid my face from you for a moment, in a surge of anger, but I will have compassion on you with my everlasting gracious love says the Lord your redeemer. For this is like the waters of Noah to me,** when I swore that the waters of Noah would never again spread over the earth; so have I sworn that I won't be angry with you again and that I won't rebuke you. (International Standard Version).

It cannot get any clearer than this. The reason why God will never again be angry with you is that he exhausted all his anger on Jesus on the cross. Isaiah 53:10-11; **"Yet it pleased the Lord to bruise him; he hath put him to grief: when thou shalt make his soul an offering for sin, he shall see his seed, he shall prolong his days, and the pleasure of the Lord shall prosper in his hand. He shall see the travail of his soul, and shall be satisfied: by his knowledge shall my righteous servant justify many; for he shall bear their iniquities"**.

God was pleased to punish Jesus for your sake; he has killed him for your sake. The sacrifice necessary for your salvation has been offered. You have been brought into the feast of celebrations, and have partaken of the meal of acceptance.

A most popular verse in scripture is John 3:16; **"For God so loved the world that He gave His only begotten Son; that whosoever believes in Him should not perish, but have Everlasting life".** This portion is much like the case of an expectant mother; she loves her child even before the child is born. She begins to make preparation for the child's coming; gets a room ready, painted with beautiful colours, and decorated with paintings and toys that will be appealing to the baby's tender mind. She shops for new clothes and shoes, diapers and several other things that the baby may never get to use, or at least not immediately. On the day of its birth, the child is born into so much love, care and attention. In the same way, God anticipates the new birth of his children; **"...that whosoever believes in him...".** But before they are born He already loves them so much; **"For God so loved the world..."** The instant a person believes in Jesus, he is born again. God now begins to manifest all the love in His heart to that new born. Some believe that after a person gets born again, God's love for them reduces; He becomes much more strict and refuses to take their nonsense. Remember, it was not because of our good works that God loved us; He loved us while we were yet sinners. We could never do enough to earn His love. **"But God has made clear his love to us, in that, when we were still sinners, Christ gave his life for us. Much more, if we now have righteousness by his blood, will salvation from the wrath of God come to us through him. For if, when we were haters of God, the death of his son made us at peace with him, much more, now that we are his friends, will we have salvation through his life"** (Romans 5:8-10. Bible in Basic English Translation.)

God will no more count your sins against you; because He no longer takes record of your sins. It is one of the blessings of our new birth. Romans 4:6-8; **"Thus David** congratulates the man and pronounces a blessing on him to whom God credits righteousness apart from the work he does. Blessed and happy and to be envied are those whose iniquities are forgiven and whose sins are covered up and completely buried. Blessed and happy and to be envied is the person of whose sin the Lord will take no account of, nor reckon it against him. (Amplified Version Classic Edition)

The cross of Jesus Christ resolved the conflict between the Love of God and the Justice of God. The conflict existed in that God being a just judge must punish sin; and that entailed the sinner dying for his sins. But God loved the sinner too much to see him die. So Jesus came and bore the anger and judgement of God; and so sin was punished on the body of Jesus. In that same act was the love of God for the sinner manifested in that the sinner is not exempted from punishment because Christ bore it in his stead. He has **"killed the fatted calf for you"**. He has now **"prepared a table**

before you in the presence of your enemies (Sin, Condemnation, Shame, Fear, Addictions, Sickness, Satan and Demons)". **Psalm 23:5.** Come and feast at His table. The Father's love for you does not diminish. It also does not increase because you do good. God unleashed the full blast of His love upon us, so He will not love us any more than He already does.

God's anger has passed over you forever. You are now the beloved of the father; and towards you, your Father is Prodigal. HALLELUYAH!!!